Visiting the Lake Di
With Your Do

Alison True

"To sit with a dog on a hillside
on a glorious afternoon
is to be back in Eden,
where doing nothing was not boring
- it was peace"

Milan Kundera

Disclaimer

Whilst every effort has been made to ensure accuracy of this walking guide at the time of publication, the author can accept no responsibility for errors, omissions or changes that may subsequently occur.

The users are advised that they are responsible for their own safety and should take measures to ensure they are properly equipped and informed. We strongly advise that an appropriate Ordinance survey map (or similar) for the area is carried with you.

No responsibility is accepted for any loss, injury or inconvenience incurred whilst using this walking guide. The owner is entirely responsible for the behaviour and safety of their dog/s.

Copyright

Design, Illustration & Artwork by Ruth Turner Designs

Published in 2012 by Nestling Publications, Keswick CA12 4TF

ISBN 9 780957 276017

Printed by
HH Reeds Printers, Southend Road, Penrith, CA11 8JH

Acknowledgements

The words thank you are not enough to convey my gratitude to all those who have assisted and supported me with the process of bringing this idea to reality. I have talked it through and shared ideas with friends, family and long suffering guests at our B&B for more than two years. Thank you all for your ideas, holiday photographs and for 'test driving' the walks for me.

An individual who deserves special mention is Joanna Hibbert, who took on a huge amount of work and used up her holidays, weekends and evenings to put my thoughts and words into legible written form. In addition she recruited her partner Alan Payton to work alongside us, not only as our photographer but so much more. Without these two I suspect the guide would never have been published.

It most certainly would not have made it into print without my husband John who has had to endure endless hours of solitude as I walked the walks or sat at my computer for days at a time. At the end of the process he simply smiled as I emptied the savings account to pay for publishing.

The concept has been very well received by 'the dog world' for want of a better description. In particular we have had wonderful support from 'Dog Friendly' who are helping to develop the concept further. I am also grateful to the Kennel Club for providing the Lanyards and publicity.

A final thank you goes to my walking companion Lucy, although she may not feel thanks are necessary as she thinks writing walk guides is brilliant fun.

Lucy is a high energy dog with a strong prey drive, and selective deafness. She taught me much about the pleasures and pitfalls of walking a dog off lead in the countryside whilst distracted by talking into a dictaphone!

Within this guide I pass on the lessons she and I learned together but also share with you some of our favourite places.

"if you eliminate smoking and gambling ......
almost all an Englishman's pleasures can be,
and mostly are, shared by his dog."

George Bernard Shaw

Introduction

The author of Dog Friendly Lake District Walks and the accompanying booklet Visiting The Lake District With Your Dog, was born and raised at Low Nest farm near Keswick in the Lake District. She and her husband, John, have owned dogs for more than twenty years and in 2006 started a dog-focussed guest accommodation business at the farm.

Her background enables Alison to give guidance appropriate to the needs of dog owners whilst being mindful of a responsibility to protect the unique landscape, the native wildlife and the livelihood of local landowners.

We are convinced that the Lake District is the most dog friendly place in Britain and no town more so than Keswick where the usual dress code is 'walking boots and a dog lead'. Dogs are welcome in many shops, some pubs and cafés, in most taxis, on all buses and even the boats on the Lakes. All of this makes it an easy and relaxed location for a dog-walking holiday.

Everything about the guide has been designed with the dog owner in mind; the information booklet to adequately prepare both dogs and owners, the walks selected and the suggested parking places to ensure that dogs are not at risk when getting out of the car. A loose-leaf format was chosen for the guide as this enables the selected route card to be carried around your neck using the pouch and lanyard supplied, leaving your hands free to hold a lead. At the time of printing all of the pubs and tea gardens mentioned have been included because they are easily accessible from the route and are genuinely dog friendly.

All of the walks feature areas that give an opportunity to run your dog off lead and many include woodland to provide shade on hot days or shelter from the rain or wind. We have also chosen walks that will provide access to water to drink, play in or for cooling off and those where, if there are stiles, they are either avoidable or easy to negotiate.

The purpose of the guide is to provide visitors to the Lake District with a range of walks that they can enjoy with their dog. It is not our intention to detail the many and varied mountain ascents as these are documented elsewhere. Where possible we have tried to offer a variety of options to allow you to tailor the walks to your ability, or that of your canine companion.

If you expect to find the walks totally flat and completely dry underfoot you could be disappointed. This is the Lake District after all; we therefore have hills and water. We have, however, tried to choose walks where the hills are minimal or the views so worth the effort that you will forgive us for including them.

Paths in the main are easy to follow and firm under foot, but there are some that have been chosen specifically to be softer on your companion's paws.

The majority of the walks are circular routes but we have included some linear routes accessed using local buses (dogs welcome). These can be approached as a days outing by walking them in their entirety or split into shorter sections as they cross bus routes. These walks are highly recommended as they offer a variety of terrain giving something for everyone and are a wonderful introduction to the area.

You will notice that several of the walks are within the same locality and some may even overlap. This is intentional and comes from understanding dog owners. The overlap enables you to become familiar with an area more quickly and thus feel more relaxed on your walk. It also enables you to adapt your walks to the needs of your dogs either linking two together for a longer walk or doing two shorter walks in one locality with a lunch break or picnic between.

As we offer various options within each walk description it is wise to read it through and find key points on the sketch map before setting out. This will enable you to decide which route you prefer and make the directions clearer during the walk.

In addition to the maps we include with the walks it is essential to carry a detailed map of the area with you if only to find a way around an obstruction, your route to the nearest hostelry or, heaven forbid, the quickest way to the Vet.

Finally, a cautionary note about the weather as the well-known phrase: "No such thing as bad weather, just wrong clothing" was surely written for the Lake District. With such a changeable climate it is possible to experience four seasons in one day, so be prepared. We would advise that whatever your plans for the day and regardless of the weather forecast you dress in layers and carry a rucksack. This enables you to add and remove clothing during your walk to keep yourself comfortable. Waterproof walking boots are also recommended.

Preparing Your Dog For A Lake District Holiday

It would be unwise to take any holiday without appropriate preparation. For you this may be breaking in a new pair of boots or, if travelling abroad, having the recommended immunisations.

Your dog cannot make its own preparations and therefore you will need to take responsibility for this. It is always wise to ensure that dogs are up-to-date with their routine vaccinations. In addition, you should consider the particular risks that may present in open countryside.

Our intention is not to worry you but to raise your awareness of potential risks in order that you can appreciate the importance of taking additional precautions.

Health care

Creepy crawlies

The majority of dog owners will know that regular worming is essential for all dogs, as canine worms can be harmful to humans. In open countryside canine worms also pose a risk to grazing livestock as they can be ingested and cause a condition known as 'Gid'. This is a serious and distressing condition as the worms migrate to the host's brain, causing fits and ultimately death. Be sure that the wormer you use is effective against canine tapeworm.

Another risk in countryside areas are tiny spider like creatures called Ticks. They live in woodland and amongst long grass and bracken. Ticks can be carried by host animals such as small rodents, sheep or deer and will attach themselves to the dog to feed on their blood. Many types of tick are harmless but some can cause mild illness, irritation or infected lumps at the bite site. A more serious disease, known as Lyme disease, can result. The symptoms of Lyme disease in dogs are loss of appetite, fever and joint stiffness.

You would be well advised to use a flea treatment that is effective against ticks within four weeks of your holiday. There are also insect repellents and garlic products said to be effective.

Even if you have used a repellent it is advisable to brush your dog outdoors on return from walks and check their ears and other skin folds where ticks may hide. A tick presses its head to the skin and inserts a probe to suck blood from the host taking on the appearance of a cyst as their body swells. To remove a tick, use a pair of tweezers or a tick remover. Take hold of it behind its head, as close to the dogs skin as possible, and pull slowly and firmly. Do not use a twisting action and do not apply pressure to the body of the tick as this can increase the risk of infection at the bite site.

As with most countryside areas in Britain there are snakes, although you are unlikely to see them. There is however a small risk that your dog may inadvertently disturb one, possibly an adder, and as a consequence get bitten. Bites are relatively unusual and rarely fatal but are an emergency requiring veterinary treatment for the pain and inflammation. It is advisable to restrict the dogs movement and keep it as calm as possible to slow the circulation of any venom.

Sore feet

A common problem amongst dogs visiting the Lake District is sore pads. The degree to which this may occur is dependant on the length of the holiday, the amount of walking you plan to do and the surfaces you walk on during your stay. Many of the natural pathways are stone and rock, as are some of the 'improved' pathways within the National Park. Sore pads will be less common in dogs who regularly do long walks or those whose walks at home involve regular 'pavement walks' where friction on the firm surface will cause the pads to thicken and harden.

If your stay in the Lake District is months or several weeks away you can limit the risk of your dog suffering with sore pads by incorporating regular walks on firm surfaces. Another option is to consider buying some boots as protection. Many varieties are now available and, although considered by some as an 'expensive gimmick', they can prevent unnecessary suffering, avoidable vet bills and disruption to your holiday plans. A period of adjustment at home in advance of your holiday is the ideal; however you will find boots readily available in pet shops or some of the outdoor shops in the Lake District towns.

Regular pavement walking on lead can also help tone muscles and strengthen your dogs' pasterns thus reducing the risk of injury. As with all exercise programmes build it up gradually and keep within the limits for age and ability.

Water safety (algae risks, swimming)

There is nothing nicer than giving your dogs the freedom to play or swim in water therefore our walks provide a great deal of opportunity for this. There are few risks associated with this activity but they are worthy of mention.

The first is 'limber tail', also known as 'dead tail'. After a period of swimming your dog may seem unable to use its tail and holds it limp. Normally all that is required is a period of rest but a veterinary opinion and some anti-inflammatory medication can be reassuring and speed recovery.

If you have a dog with a strong desire to chase it can be wise to keep them on a long lead or distract their attention when there are waterfowl on or close to the shores of the larger lakes. Some dogs just won't give up the chase and will swim out in pursuit to a point where they are well out of their depth and at considerable risk if they tire.

In prolonged periods of dry weather when the water level in the Lakes is low and the rivers are shallow and slow running (unusual for the Lake District !) there can be a risk of high levels of Blue Green algae. Signs will usually be erected quite quickly in affected areas, but if you are concerned it is best to err on the side of caution and keep your dogs (and yourselves) out of the water.

The algae form into clumps knows as blooms. These can be visible close to the shoreline and can have a musty odour. In some cases the water takes on a green-blue appearance looking similar to oil on water.

Choosing holiday accommodation

You will find the Lake District to be a genuinely dog friendly place to stay. Dogs are welcome in many shops, pubs, cafés, buses, taxis, boats on the Lakes, and even the narrow gauge railway at Ravenglass.

There are many guest houses, hotels, camp sites and self-catering cottages where dogs are welcome but do check their 'dog friendly' credentials with the owner before booking. We have heard of places advertising as 'dog friendly' where dogs are expected to sleep in your car parked in the street, or where you have to walk ten minutes to the park to toilet your dog, which is no fun in the wee small hours.

On arrival at your accommodation, if the information is not readily available, remember to ask for details of the local vet. If you ask you won't need them but Murphy's Law says if you don't ask you might!

Get in training

People want different things from their dogs but most expect to have a degree of control over the dog's behaviour in given situations. There is no pleasure in spending all your time on a walk nagging your dog to 'heel' so it is worth taking the time to train your dog to walk sensibly on a lead. Also training a sit and wait on lead can assist you during tricky parts of a walk, or allow others to pass on a narrow path. Distance commands such as wait and recall can be incredibly useful in maintaining control when your dog is off lead and a 'fast down' command can be a life saver.

There are a variety of walking aids that will give you more control than a standard collar and lead, including chest harnesses or head collars. Again, these are available locally but getting your dog used to them for short periods in advance of your trip is time well spent.

Should you be unable to trust your dog 'off lead', you may find a flexi lead, training lead or long line useful. These allow your dog to enjoy a little more freedom and enable you to negotiate any tricky areas more safely. (See photo)

A training lead has the added advantage of enabling you to walk with your dog on lead but 'hands free' by securing it around your waist. This is especially useful if you need to check a map, steady yourself or if you want to use walking poles. (See photo)

Lost dogs

Having your dog within sight is not only the best way to keep them out of trouble but also the most reliable way of ensuring that they will not get lost. Always keep one eye on your dog and the other on the horizon scanning for potential risks (livestock/ wildlife/ bicycles/ children).

It is a legal requirement for all dogs to wear a collar and identification disc but as you are away from home it is useful to add another contact number too. Suggestions are a mobile number (but remember reception is poor in parts of the Lake District), your holiday accommodation or a family member who knows how to contact you.

Wearing a second identification tag has additional benefits too as it will jangle when your dog moves. This gives animals an early warning of your dogs approach and also means that you can hear where your dog is if obscured from view by trees or bracken.

It is wise to have your dog registered with a national database by means of micro-chipping or tattoo as this ensures the best chance of re-uniting you if you do lose him. Don't forget to update your details on the registers if you have moved house.

Enjoying the countryside with your dog

Many dog owners regularly enjoy country walks with their dogs. However, we are aware that for some of you this may be a new experience or that your country walks may be restricted to country parks, where you may not encounter the same range of situations.

We encourage all visitors to this wonderful area to act responsibly. In all aspects of life there are a few people who do not and as a result spoil the enjoyment of others.

There is so much more to being a responsible dog owner than picking up after your dog, but let's just dwell on that briefly. The local authorities do not make it easy for us by providing disposal bins as happens in most urban areas. The expectation is that you will pick it up and carry it home for disposal. However, if you see a public waste bin en route you may use this. Accepted means of disposal is to 'double bag' if using standard dustbins.

Alternatively there are a variety of 'carry home' pouches for used bags, or you could use a drawstring travel water bowl as we do. These are more discreet and easy to carry; and, as they are waterproof, can be washed out or disinfected. Another option is to have a dedicated outer pocket in your rucksack or, better still, buy your dog a rucksack so that he can carry it himself !

You should pick up everywhere in the Lake District. Please do not think "it's biodegradable", "it's just like sheep poo", "it can't matter out here"... if nothing else just think for a moment where it may end up; you leave it on the fell side, it's eaten by a sheep, you tuck into a lamb shoulder from the specials board in the pub after your long walk – need I say more?

The walks we have detailed in our publications are designated footpaths, and we would urge you to keep to these where possible. Farmers are not miserable killjoys, but ask you to keep to the paths to protect their land and their livestock. On lowland walks it can be tempting to stray from the footpaths as open fields can be viewed as 'just grass'. Most of us would appreciate that we could not expect to wander with gay abandon through a field of cabbages, but do not appreciate that grassland in the Lake District is a valuable 'crop'. It is grazing land and, in the summer months, may be grown to provide hay and silage crops to feed the farm livestock through the winter. Flattening the grass crop onto the ground inhibits its growth, makes it difficult to mow and often causes it to rot.

There are certain periods and circumstances when you are required to keep your dog on a fixed lead, but this can, in some situations, be up to two metres in length (see www.countrysideaccess.gov.uk) These periods are often related to times and situations where there may be ground nesting birds such as open fell side or meadow. A tell tale sign is birds rising from the ground and flying just a short distance away or even feigning injury to draw you away from the site of their nest. If you see this odd behaviour you should put your dog on a lead until you leave that area.

Safety around wild animals and farm livestock

The biggest bone of contention with regards to dog walking in the countryside is the risk of dogs chasing livestock. As dog owners we alone are responsible for ensuring that our dog never has the opportunity to do so.

You will know that dogs should be kept under close control, preferably on a lead, when near livestock. You should also be aware that if a farmer considers your dog to be causing harm to his livestock he is, in the eyes of the law, justified in shooting your dog. This very rarely happens but none of us would want to take such a risk with our beloved pet.

The dog in the picture lives on a farm and walks amongst sheep daily. She is 100% reliable off lead with them but does chase deer/rabbit/ducks/pheasant/crows, and would scatter sheep in all directions if they happened to get in her way. Technically she is not chasing the sheep but would still be causing anxiety and potential harm therefore it is best for all concerned to keep her on her lead in such situations.

Even the best-behaved dog can produce panic in a flock or an individual sheep. Should the sheep start to run just stand still so that they can see you are no threat. Once they are calm you may quietly continue your walk. This is particularly important during the time when sheep are 'in lamb' or at lambing time. As these periods vary throughout the National Park it is wise to ask when you book your holiday or on arrival at your destination.

Another occurrence which hits the headlines on the rare occasion that it happens is injury, or even death, caused by cattle. The general rule is that if you feel at all uneasy you should not enter the field where there are cattle. This is one good reason to be sure you have a map with you, as you may need to find a detour to complete your planned walk rather than having to retrace your steps.

When you have a dog with you, it is the dog that will get the cows' interest. In most circumstances cattle will pay you little attention; they see walkers pass them every day. Keep your dog close to you and walk quietly and calmly through the area. However, if you feel uncomfortable put a greater distance between you and the animals by straying off the path and following the boundary of the field. Most farmers would much prefer this to having a serious incident with his livestock.

Should you feel in any way threatened by the situation you MUST unleash your dog and make your own 'escape' your priority. Your dog can move out of danger more quickly and will take the focus off you as you leave the immediate area.

A hidden risk is deer that may frequent the woodland, especially the deeper, denser areas of forest although they can also be found grazing on the fells. You are unlikely to see them and they are rarely a problem unless your dog has a strong hunting instinct. The only advice we can give is to allow your dog the freedom to run but keep them within sight so that you can call them back quickly if they pick up a scent.

The rutting season is October and November so this is when the males will be most feisty and potentially would challenge a dog. The fawns will be born in May or June and will be quite vulnerable for their first few weeks of life. If you see a deer running off but keeping you in view or looking back intermittently she has a fawn hidden nearby. You must put your dog on a lead and move out of the area. It is wise, even demanded in some woodland, to keep dogs on a lead during the breeding season.

The Maverick Herdwick

In fairness the trait we are about to describe is not exclusive to the Herdwick, the 'native' breed in the Lake District, but is probably in evidence in all sheep to some degree.

People go to great lengths to 'sheep proof' their dogs and can confidently walk through sheep grazing areas without the dog showing any interest at all. The problem we find is with the Maverick Herdwick whose sole purpose in life appears to be to get dogs into bother.

They scale walls, break through fences and ford streams to get themselves into places they really aren't supposed to be; merely, we feel, to spoil your day. They will lurk in the bracken on seemingly sheep-free fell sides or hide behind trees in the woods and await their quarry, no doubt sniggering under their breath. At the very moment you turn your attention away from your dog, the maverick leaps out and all hell breaks loose!

You may not see them but always assume that they may be hiding just around the next bend. Our advice is to relax and enjoy exploring the beautiful walks but by keeping your dog in view you can spoil the maverick's game.

Guide Book Terminology

Beck – small river.

Crag – a steep sided rocky outcrop often dropping into the valley below.

Gates – please be sure that you close gates firmly behind you.

There are several types of gate along the paths in the national park:

Five bar gate – We use the term to mean a large, farm style gate as seen within field boundaries. In reality these can often have 6 or even 7 bars.

Kissing gate – refers to a small gate which swings between a narrow fenced area, opening and closing to allow one person to pass through.

Wicket gate – a small wooden pedestrian gate on a footpath.

Intermittently grazed – We use this term throughout the guide to alert you to areas which may be grazed by sheep or cattle. As stock is moved regularly this does not mean that there will be livestock, only that you must check before allowing your dog off lead and remain alert to this potential hazard within that area.

Off lead – when we use this term we do not mean allow your dog to run amok like a thing possessed but let him run freely within sight and sufficiently close that you maintain adequate control.

Paths – In this guide we refer to various common path surfaces:

Forest Track – generally quite wide with a surface of compacted gravel or hardcore. Firm under foot and ideal on wet days.

Improved pathway – mostly found on heavily used routes. These have been laid with stone to stop erosion of the land. They are firm under foot but can be slippery when wet.

Multi user path – the old railway line from Keswick to Threlkeld and the path along the east shore of Thirlmere. These are broad paths of compacted gravel which are used by walkers and cyclists.

Woodland paths – usually well trodden but can be quite rough with rocks and tree roots. May be slippery when wet.

Please note that some smaller pathways on hills can resemble stream beds in wet weather as the water finds a natural route downhill.

Paw rating – Routes are scored according to how dog friendly they are. Points are lost for static hazards such as stiles but also for variable hazards such as livestock consequently a 3 paw walk could infact be a 5 paw walk if completely stock free.

Soft under foot – can mean meadow grass, open fell of rough grasses and mud paths or, on some fell tops, ankle deep peat bog.

Tarn – a small lake or large fresh water pool on the fells.

Terrace walk – a roughly horizontal path partway up the fellside.

Woods and Forests – we use the term forest for woods that have been planted by man and wood for naturally occurring woodland areas of broad leaf trees.

Dog Friendly Lake District Walks publication

Dog friendly Lake District Walks is intended as an 'add to' series of walks specifically chosen for dog walkers. Your initial purchase includes:

- The information booklet entitled "Visiting the Lake District with your dog" which is packed with useful information to make your stay easier and more enjoyable;
- A ring binder with capacity to add further walks from the series or your own favourites;
- A PVC pouch and lanyard to enable you to carry the route card with you while leaving your hands free to hold a dog lead;
- Details of dog friendly tea gardens, pubs and hotels easily accessible from each walk route;
- A map showing the location of the dog friendly places to eat;
- Route maps which identify other car parks to allow you to drive to other locations from which you can devise your own short walks;
- Detailed walk routes all with variations to allow you to tailor the walk to your ability. In addition we mention other 5 paw walks that you can easily follow without a route description. This results in a large number of walk options within in each series, as an example series one introduces you to more than 30 options;
- Contact details are included for local Vets and pet shops.

The initial series of walks is based within the north of the Lake District National Park. Research has already begun to find walks with similar qualities within the other areas of the National Park; Central, South, East and West.

Once you have a starter pack all you need to do is purchase the additional pack of walks to add to your binder, over time building up a comprehensive guide of some of the best walks we can find.

Future walks in the series will become available through our dedicated website. Should you wish to be notified when these become available please use the e-mail facility on our website: **www.dogfriendlylakedistrictwalks.co.uk**

Cumbria Coast and Forests

Cumbria Forests

There are several forests within the Lake District National Park which have a variety of routes that cater for all abilities.

These are:

Whinlatter Forest Park, near Keswick. Grid reference: NY209245

Dodd Wood, near Keswick. Grid reference: NY 234283

Dunnerdale Forest, near Ulpha. Grid reference: SD228977

Ennerdale Forest, Ennerdale valley. Grid reference: NY109153

Greystoke Forest, *Greystoke*, near Penrith. Grid reference: NY403347

Grizedale Forest, near Hawkshead. Grid reference: SD336944

Cumbria Coast

The Cumbria coast is not within the National Park but easily accessible from it.

http://www.coastradar.com/ search site for Cumbria, then place name.

Allonby. A small seaside village with easy access to the sands (north section is quieter)

Drigg. Access down a country lane. Long stretch of beach with dunes and nature reserve.

Haverigg (nr Millom). North of the village, near Rugby club is best. Large area of dunes.

Maryport. Best access is south of the harbour. Coastal park here if the tide is in.

St Bees. The best beach on the North West coast. Little there when the tide is in.

Seascale. A small coastal town. Dogs welcome on the beach but not the green alongside.

Local Information

Pet shops in the Lake District

Podgy Paws, Keswick. CA12 5AS.	017687 73737
Paws by the Lake, Waterhead, Ambleside, Cumbria. LA22 0EZ.	015394 32014
Lamberts Pet Supplies, 1 Albert Road, Grange-Over-Sands, LA11 7EZ.	015395 36544

Vets accessible from the Lake District and Cumbria

Oak Hill, Lake Road Windermere Cumbria, LA23 2EQ.	015394 88555 015394 42859
Oak Hill, Church Street, Ambleside, LA22 0BU.	015394 32631
Paragon, Newbiggin, Nr Penrith, CA11 0HT.	01768 483789
Millcroft, Southey Hill, Keswick, CA12 5NR.	017687 72590
Millcroft, Wakefield Road, Cockermouth, CA13 0HR.	01900 826666
West Lakeland St Bridgets Lane, Egremont, CA22 2BB.	01946 820312
Browne & McKinney, Church St, Broughton-in-Furness, LA20 6HJ.	012297 16230
South Lakes Veterinary Centre,Victoria Rd, Ulverston, LA12 0BY.	01229 582900
Archway Veterinary Practice, Station Square, Grange-over-Sands, LA11 6EH.	015395 32669

Other Important / Useful Information

Health - NHS direct **0845 4647** 24hrs service - will give details of the most appropriate service near to your location.

Emergency services - Mountain rescue / Coast guard – **999** ask for Police and they will alert the appropriate organisation.

Weather report - **0844 846 2444** www.lakedistrictweatherline.co.uk

Accommodation - Cumbria Tourism: **01539 822222.** Web: www.golakes.co.uk